IN NO ONE'S LAND

IN NO ONE'S LAND

PAIGE ACKERSON-KIELY

AHSAHTA PRESS

BOISE STATE UNIVERSITY · BOISE · IDAHO · 2007

Ahsahta Press, Boise State University
Boise, Idaho 83725
http://ahsahtapress.boisestate.edu

Copyright © 2007 by Paige Ackerson-Kiely
Printed in the United States of America
Cover design by Quemadura
Book design by Janet Holmes
First printing January 2007
Second printing March 2009
ISBN-13: 978-0-916272-92-0

Library of Congress Cataloging-in-Publication Data

Ackerson-Kiely, Paige, 1975-
In no one's land / Paige Ackerson-Kiely.
   p. cm.
ISBN-13: 978-0-916272-92-0
I. Title.

PS3601.C56I5 2007
811'.6—dc22
                          2006016615

ACKNOWLEDGMENTS

Bellingham Review ("Interrogation," "Greenland"); *Court Green* ("Safety in Numbers"); *jubilat* ("To the Understudy," "The Potential of Rapture," "From the Understudy"); *Ninth Letter* ("Foreplay," "Instructional Lecture for a Liquor Store Clerk"); *Pleiades* ("Prayer for Singularity," "Shepherding"); *Spinning Jenny* ("Dear Guest").

The epigraph by Bertel Gripenberg translates as "In no one's land, with no one will I stay."

Christopher;

Contents

I intet land, hos ingen vill jag stanna.

—Bertel Gripenberg

"In no country of no one I want to stay"

Swedish

Foreplay

You are sitting on the bed. The motel room is the color of breastmilk, nutritive water rinsing the palate of you. The sheets are not soft reminders of human capacity for forgiveness with their random tufts like a father roughing up his boy's hair; *son you've made me proud*. There are times when an absence of pride means the lion is eating his cub. The lioness under some reeds growling like an unwound basket. Unthreading stalks like tight stitches in all the wounds you don't mean to make, then abandon, embarrassed. Here is a man darning his sock. Here is a woman spitting into a sink. Here is all of Berlin in the creosote of the coughing, sitting primly at the windowsill, looking out. You lean back on the bed which is like curling into a giant yawn; pretty, ambivalent shrug. Any minute now someone will push his way through the door and announce something. Dinner is served. The surgery was a great success. I'm sorry ma'am, but you'll have to come with me. Answer a few questions.

Instructional Lecture
for a Liquor Store Clerk

The customers want something from you that you do not own but in fact lord over. Let the older men call you baby or hon, it relaxes them. See how they tremble, hands like a wet fawn one hour old pushing up to stand. It will be a hard winter and the fawn won't make it. Mostly it is bleak. Once in a while a customer won't have enough money and you will have to make a call. Will they return later and pay gratefully. Will they never return, like the buck in November cruising the knotweed. The bright orange cap in the bush looks like a loud, upside-down tureen to you, but to the buck it has a grayscale wash that is easy to ignore. Someday you will die, this always surprises you. Usually customers do have the money but sometimes they will cough into their hands as they present it. Chronic Wasting Disease has affected herds in the Midwest, but so far it is pretty safe around here. Drooping head or ears, tremors, stumbling, increased salivation, and excessive thirst and urination. There is a gun under the cash register but you won't have to use it. In fact earlier, when I said *lord over,* I was speaking of benevolence. If you hit a doe with your car, and she crumpled into a ditch but her eyes were still open, her eyes open like a small child drawing a picture of dark roses, would you shoot her? Lastly, when making change remember to smile. Your smile is resplendent.

Nocturne IV

Night is a wheelchair
and the wheel cock-eyed.
I feel strongly about fireflies
and am lining up the mayonnaise jars.
It goes like this,
night does, excuse to get somewhere
not directly.
I love our children sleeping
in dens of sour breath
and the curtain red and slightly parting.
Baby, this. All of the shadows
are hands beckoning rain and rain again.
All of the tendrilled, mounting dark.
You weren't anywhere I was planning to go.
The path from the porch to the car
for example, feeling my way along.

Dear Guest

The leaves are only leaves
& the house is stationary
when you say small I am warm,

(O JJ Cale help me fetch that nickel
from your larynx) & let me touch myself
for the celebrity I just missed.

The leaves are only leaves tonight
I am a guest in my idea to lie across
the tight machine that holds us so apart.

Whoever you are (winnowing in North Dakota)
whoever you are (ciphering in Denmark)
your hand will not stay with me in spite

of my own hand (wrist that circles the
Arctic Circle) and the leaves are unfortunately
incalculable from the dozen or so vernaculars.

Love Letter

I told you my apartment number; I gave you a description of the way water comes out of my kitchen faucet, crippled sluicing thing. There is no incidence to speak of. Few reasons I could give for all this lonesome paperwork. When I need you you don't come running. When my head bends its soft web to the ground, when the ground appears ready to listen. My name is twenty-four letters long plus seventy-two words for snow. On the top left-hand corner of every sheet of paper I draw a picture of a hollow log and a pillow, black from bogwater, at one end.

Illness

Men looking down
at their wristwatches
take notice.

Gray goes
the evening indistinguishable
gray goes
the kindling;
piece of finessed handicraft.
All of the ways
you have practiced
sadness
in front
of a mirror mouthing
whatever,
gray.

So that the last woman
left
in the bar
is the same woman
in the bar earlier,
saying
yeah, I've got some abandonment issues.

Snow
falling and melting

[continued]

on a dumpster out back
really
shining in the moonlight.

People who say, at least
I have my health.

Other people nodding.

From the Understudy

If you would look at me I would show you something. The size of it, ask any man and it is this big. I don't really know what interests you, but by watching the tick of your wrist by your side I could drum up a thousand doves assured over Palestine, beaks tweaking it is yours, undoubtedly. What mine. Dovecote. White woolen snow a shameful cage on the ground. Grass bent in grief owned by this sharecropper. Knock knock who's there? The door is a trestle and the water's low. My love's a gothic push straight out of the University of Chicago. I should have asked your name. I should have said your name out loud and answered yes?

Shepherding

Mild lamb, I would
gather so closely to me.
I raise my hand,
ask to be chosen.
Life was interesting
when I believed everything
I heard. Now
there is wool in my ear canal.
I give myself away.
Take this hay, take this
big heap of wet hay
in your pitchfork.
Move it somewhere else.
There is plenty of room
in the field. I smoke
behind the fencepost.
I know clearly that I will
remove my pants
when it is requested
I remove my pants.
They will call all of us in
on cold nights,
though no one calls
to me specifically.

Leave the Job That Is No Lover

Touch a job and it will grow big. Touch it into a puddle of paperwork or a sky looming, you piece of typical loam. Bury your rubbish. Touch product, touch money that does not mean your driveway will get plowed after the next snowstorm. Touch the collars of strange men, adjust them. When you are alone, touch yourself as though someone is watching a boy chase a grocery bag as it blows up and off the sidewalk, lands briefly at his feet, suggesting it might be caught. It won't. Touch the poor woman with her change laid out like pieces of a broken wristwatch. Put them together without shame. Touch your forehead to your desk, be the plastic smell of the Xerox machine, the Band-Aid that is dirty and won't stay in place replicating itself until you are covered in Band-Aids but must keep slapping them down. They want, like you, to come off. Touch the note from your boss thatbegins: Refuse delivery of… Customers come in wearing sunglasses. Be discerning when you check yourself out. Ask, can I help you? Again. Now ask it again. Ask it until your voice loses its lace, no one should hear panties in your voice. You are a hero, heroes help others. Touch the sleeve of your sweater and pull it over your weaker hand. When your shift is done go home alone. After you lock up, pause to touch the door like it is someone's wife. Say, he never stopped loving you. Walk toward your parked car, shrugging into the cold. Keep walking.

Brother

You might not know him
the way a cattle car fills
& empties dyingly
while you grab the hand
next to you & watch
the progression of cattle
the way they halt on the ramp
like when you discover your blouse
has become unbuttoned
& must turn away
& in doing so forget
the placement of words
or the forgiveness of strangers.

You may not have seen him
the way you have seen a girl
leaning against a brick government
building, trying to light a cigarette
as snow mounts in not the way
babies are made from a mounting
shielding her face with her hands.

You could be some white chick
over-smiling in an elevator
of strangers.

[continued]

Someone in distress. Someone
yelling get him off of me.

You might never get him off of you.

Deer Population at Night

Deer at the roadside, deer in the meadow,
tall grass, headlight. Broken, bro. ken, when

divided brother, to know.

Where they roam. Where their small hooves
scrape. You want me to write them out?
Say the forest is on the next page, scatter?

Who among us will take on their lean peril,
who has a face that is running away,
a soft hock asking to be engaged, please

leave me alone with my fear.

As if you can know them by where they fall.

How they roll precisely from the windshield
the windshield with now precise cracks--
behind it you cry for only yourself.

The sheer numbers acquit you,
turn away from your glib matter while
quietly the stars undress in the dark,
(there are thousands, thousands). The right
rustle sends the doe bounding from her fawn;
you never call your mother anymore.   *[continued]*

Forget it, you know and don't, so ordinary

how many there are. The dark.

A Moment as Roscoe Holcomb

Sadness is the boarded-up mill turning in my wrist.
Take me to the garden. Let me kill the livestock.

One by one mason jars are filled;
my beet-struck heart vinegared.

Everywhere I go, the casual brides.
The farmers lowering down on their elbows.

Angles in my narrow voice--
who has filched all of these round feelings,

the hapless skirts limp on the line:
no need to call in sick.

Nights from now I will join the river.
I will say current and it will be mine,

as a man turned away at the door.
In the meantime, at least, work.

Mice nesting in the walls,
rust dolefully eating the edges.

On the Gentle Nature of Swales

You are eclipsed by mountains. You are the low down moaning of a blues song. Every night a shepherd leads his flock down the leeward side. When you moved into a farmhouse 31 miles from here your heart was suddenly a ripe apple and you felt the animals holding your gaze, the barn across the way your own sweltering podium. Something is always burning inside of you; it is not terrible to burn. In the Autumn they douse the prairie with fire to encourage next years crop. From the farm you wrote: when I used to live in the Mountains. Used is one word that makes me tired. It is almost like lying down. The livestock, to whom you tip your feedcap. Say, lie down sweetheart. Some animals will. Once, when you were in our kitchen and I could only hear your padding and murmur like a soft wind over swales, I wanted to lie down forever. To finally unstrap from my skin and rise up as soft smoke the way I read it might happen. Rise up. You write you have a breath-taking view of the mountains from your back window.

Spring Thaw

Spring with your disheveled mouths beginning
to open. Glad I am for doorways.
For a simple frame.

In winter I allow you to guess correctly
that I was sleeping. The paw of me
placed over the snout of me. My friends
the dead flowers in a windowbox
nowhere I knew where my friends were.

I allow you to guess correctly. The confidence
you will gain will make speaking—
a tomcat sprays the dogwood—blooming.

Hello. I was forgotten. When my jaw at first
unlocks I will say no one has loved me as much.

Foucault's Bed

The sheets are at once an amalgam, half-precious. The sheets are Kandinsky's concentric circles and the square is a bed, usual as an eight-year old's day. Mostly the sheets are a pasture eaten to nubs with the hay breath of horses still lingering and the farrier in the stalls hammering blackly. Foucault did it, died he did. I was busy asking for something. All the swales of you I have to pan out to love; moles and lesions against a white backdrop. Where heaven is the climax. Get up, go to work like you are a dentist and everyone's scared. The bed is where your work, castigated, is not like two mares staring down the girder of their noses. Barring wild horses, who will have to be put down, Foucault might've added. Crawl or jump in, death just makes the other saddest. Woe. Like what you would say to horses if you ever wanted them to stop.

Privacy

Nobody here.
Nobody like rivers
gouge you the way
to needs fro
and the blonde children
sleeping in the grass
with their simple closing
know when to shut-up
you better.
The river is alone
in it's spilling
our father's aboveall
face another pool
we hate and hate
when we occur to it,
a thousand our fathers
wooden matryoshkas—
you want the smallest one
that does not open.

Prayer for Singularity

Our father the interminable
The sick but not too bad
The low lying cot our father

The floodplain, the single drought
The woman crying in her

Bra the woman crying our
Father
Who art

Says the undergrad--

I slept with him and him--
Slept away

The father art
A picnic table
And a son standing awkwardly   to the side

With a daisy in his hand. A daisy
Flimsy on its stalk

Walking by your apartment every day.
Are you home

Four walls someone saying   *[continued]*

There has to be love there to
Call it

Hello? Hello.
It's me, our
Father

The gusto. Thy plate after plate
Cleared our
Father

Fathers feathers hollowed
And brushed back
Vainly

At least 20 minutes a day
In the bathroom come
Shooting

up Father

Is he red and dead
Done father,

whose art
Is simply not your name.

The Potential of Rapture

I locked up all
of the beautiful things
that might move me.

The bell around a dark ankle
turning and turning.

A stranger smiles.
Her face is no curling-up
in bed.

If I knew the world was going
to end, I'd just run out into
the street and fuck the first
chick I saw, says
a teenage virgin.

Where you go when you are scared

that we might have the verdant
and the humid. Friendly air.
People meaning their handwaves.
An answer is the way you can jump
from a ledge equal to your height
without getting hurt.
Your home.
Every pane of glass

[continued]

someone laid on their precious
breath. There.
Or there.

Boy I am
leaving too many rooms
for the crowded street. Lay
down your sweet head
for now

to know as we do know
to know. To know
one damn thing.

To the Understudy

It is true I am afraid of the stranger in men.

On the Internet some woman kneeling
provocatively.

O one of many crickets
I crumpled into toilet paper,
deafening.

Where are the lacy
Christening gowns. The babies
leaning headstrong.

Took a walk in my neighborhood
past the church. Touched
the freshly painted siding, my side
that said sit down girlfriend.

Sidle up and let's watch
the traffic like faces for
confirmation.

The night sky that does not
twinkle, the headlights
one

after another   *[continued]*

not friendly eyes
averting.

I know I will probably die
with no one
around. I'm not sick or
anything

like that—
there they go. There they go again.

Safety In Numbers

Gaza City a pair of old shoes
one left out to dry.

In the park, a couple folding
into each other. A single
swan preening his feathered
chest. Mites, then none.

To love and buy a scarf.
To have a Winter
by the side of someone
having a Winter.

Is a radiator hissing sad.
A radiator in a weekend home.
It is Tuesday,

trapped on an ark with
a small family
and tons of animals.

Come the unrain,
multiplying.

I'll take as many
as you can spare.

Topologies

Can I come inside

wanted to say the big
dumb man of me.

Wanted again to defend all
big dumb indoor things.
A column fan
in the closet. Knotted
orange electrical cord pressed
against the chest defensively.

To need to be pushed inside
of something to become
alive.

I stood outside in the rain and
the mudroom
grew lonely as salt
cast over the agitated back
of a pregnant woman
only invited to dinner
in case there was
too much drinking &
vacuumed up later by
a homely waitress who
will never land a part.

The fields to the left and right
full of glassy blackbirds
resting,

each thing subtracted becomes ever
ominous.

I love you
love you

you

No, I've Had Enough

From the bow of my boat I daydream your pants, the longing is so great that I might imagine slipping into them, not just a hand but both legs. I might take a jog around the deck so great is my desire to not just touch you but to dwell righteously in your femur, which is hot like a fever but in the end is not a fever. Jesus came and he kissed the eyes of a blind woman. Jesus opened his robe and the ocean poured forth. Look closely at all of the fish we have to eat, their scales upon which the keys of our teeth may finally sing. Their bones a most staunch crunch to remind us now, right now, get down on your knees and put your hands over your ears and become as small as you possibly can, c'mon, you can fit into that shoebox with the balled up tissue paper lying next to you smelling like Cambodian food. And Jesus came with food to Cambodia and elsewhere he came with plates of pickerel and snapper and cod and jellyfish. The world is limp and furthermore dead and I am so hungry I will not eat a single thing as you are everything to me, you are at this instant every single thing.

Cavalry Men

To date, I am surrounded.

The meadow larks with their incessant
jingle, the grass with its needs.

The sky moaning,
put a shirt on and face me.

I know there are men in the distance.
They rustle as though braiding

their wives' fine hair.
I am an ugly woman.

I know there are men in the distance.
The trees at the edge of the woods

are sacrificing one another.
Who will be the first to fall in a storm

I do not know.
I do know this.

The horses they ride have stopped speaking—
shame is not a silent bride

rolling her eyes at a fitting.
The eyes of the horses

are wet as though nursed upon
and their long faces, clutched.

I will never marry.
This gets me.

Onenightstand

Touch me not, I have one long headache. And clothe me not in cool tones which sicken the complexion until my skin hangs with trepidation over my boots over the parking lot over the miles of grass, dead and ugly and astute in its finality. Teach me not of kindness, tell me not of gnomes picking through the hair of other gnomes. I want no intimate thing; I am frightened of the intimate thing. The hand I might clasp, the stranger's hand with blue veins spreading out like meth in a small town, the hand I would clasp as a plane was going down, down, a child digging to China, past the hot center where anger was, then sadness, then uncontainable sadness. Explain to me not the crust of the earth, the cool skin of the body, which is beautiful because it is the largest organ, all glockenspiel on overture. Do it to me over and over, the way an explorer pours himself into the map of his conquest until he becomes north, a cherub to his side drawing breath from his ear. Do it not for the deer with their eyes like the bedrooms of unrented apartments. Tell me how you set out the salt-lick when you were a boy. Tell me how they approached your hand, which you pretended held food, but was merely a closed fist.

On the Austerity of Autumn

Falling leaves are not dancing and the crow is no counselor apparent as a cast-iron pot. It feels shitty, all this negating but I am quitting Romance—no estranged glances cast over the prow and the lake, just blue and ordinarily still lest we be swallowed and drowning lonely. That was the time I wanted to kiss someone deeply and it was forbidden. Treading water. God was shiny and dwelled peacefully in the village fertilizing crops and carrying planes in the stave of his hand to gentle landings at the Burlington Airport. This is the time I hold the railing as I make my way downstairs. Omit clutch. Omit grasp and falter. I am through painting lakes disguising green algae. Through with nights meting out the unhavables, the insects multiplying symphonically in the yard. It would be impolite to say fucking. I won't. It is Autumn and soon it will be Winter.

One Type of Hunger

It is October, an October said low under a light meant to resemble candlelight. Pretty. The leaves do their best to hang on; no one goes to the store until there is no choice. The refrigerator is empty. A man leaves the house. A man folds his hands together flush as a door clicked shut. A man. Leaves. Falling is not the first step of a child; doesn't begin. Yards and yards of dead and curling mouths. A man is known by his hunger, the way he tilts his head to the side, at once admonishing and at once a boy hoarding junk. The way a man falls and breaks badly. Each bone a hopeful twig laddered to another hopeful twig, posed skyward. October and the leaves are reorganized first by color and then by who dies first. We let the dark ones die alone. Nightcry. Trunks bellowing then starving in a proven mouthlessness. Where is the man. Nothing comes up from the ground, the ground is afghaned and unseen. Where has the man gone.

Command of Material Goods

Every day the napkin
asks me for the fork.
The napkin is glad;
the napkin is waiting.
An estranged husband
asks the clerk for the
newspaper. She glibly
points nowhere, says:
Over there. A voice
meant for only you
is a hymn. You
are Jerusalem—
over there. Is
instruction enough.
I laid in the meadow.
I covered my body
with birdseed.
Still, birds did not
come to feed
on my body.
Finally, my solemn shoes
murmured: stand up.
Stand up now please
you joyful, joyful thing.

Different Kinds of Clean

It is nothing to say I am
nothing and slink out the door.

Some men spend time with themselves
every morning, say, I made myself thus
for you I am made.

To pick absently at the lint. To have a lot
of work to do.

My hand will find any hand in the dark
it suffices. As a kid I busted my ass
cleaning my father's place, clean
and erotically so, I could have said
so clean you can eat off it,
but you don't.

Some men make a gesture of peace
by rocking back on their heels and placing
their hands in pockets.
Most stuff you should hide. Kids know this,
babies. It is my nature to steal.
Clean and raw nature the wind
takes the dust. Don't leave. Or better yet

there is a lady you can hire for that
and she's cheap.

Open Letter to Cy Twombly

Every eye that you see is a crate
slung open. When as a girl I
picked flowers till the neighbor
rushed at me looking down.
The whole world is a handkerchief
where in the desert it stays dry
but dirty, no one cries, no one
cries rightfully.
In Olympia I saw the corner, tiny
embroidered edelweiss an old bag
dragged the needle in and out
too nostalgic to drop crooked stitch
dead—the cloth in Olympia sodden.
How in a rain it is instinct
to lower your lids, or in the bath.
Helen Keller did not close her eyes
as the water ladled so from
mother's fine preening hands.
Though I was not there to see it
I read, her mother carefully wiped
the water from little Helen's little
open eyes and knew something
was up. It would be appropriate
to tell you that the flowers I
picked soon closed, folding inside
of themselves in thirsty masturbation
and quite embarrassed. No matter

how many times I see anything
never learn to be just nice.

Defining Moments

Over 2.5 million years the glaciers
loved and left the earth 15 times.

Some nights you sleep with a pillow.

Nights you do not sleep with a pillow.

What sacred book you pry from a stranger
you've become mere.

Nickels are worthless.

Give it two weeks and that waxwing'll
be out of here.

Overweight children cache
of spent cartridges draw on a dark
mustache with that finepoint.

Good people, raise your cameras.

Homicidal Ballad

Mostly we kill for love.

I was so hungry
either unzipping pants
like a hard rain raws
the foxglove
or rummaging
the cabinet blindly.

Packet of jerky
& the man who holds
the packet against his haunch—
some pierced
quixotic gentler of
jerky.

Was all there was.

Driving whatever through
the night of you
driving right on through
wanting a reason to stop
and say:

Man, I could stay
here forever.

I moved on, full morning wake
followed by wake I wanted
to stop, shut out the light damn
I should
have

cut the lights
slowed down at least

left the car running
with its vents yammering
warmer,
warmer still.

An Old Recording

The shape of our affair
was edged with tin
and sung in Bulgarian
by scarved women,
conducted by a Russian man.
It was heard once
on a treeless hill in Torshavn
by a child who was yelled
at twice already that day—
once for cutting his mother's
business cards into triangles
and letting them into the wind,
and the other time
for something he can't remember
and won't.
But when he calls his father
long distance
to Helsinki where father flies
for a commercial jet-liner,
he hears father's
spatula hands
scoop up the newspaper
while the boy
reports, my teacher's voice
sounds like apples crunching or
the weather is gray as a trenchcoat
forgotten on a sinking ship.

Mm-hmm. Yes. Go on.
The noise
of the newspaper rustling
is father's way of
keeping abreast for his boy,
staying in touch
with the boy who does not
yet live in a world of newspapers
or the sound they sometimes make—
like I love you whispered
over and over until
the awkward place which is neither
the ear or the throat itches terribly
and cannot be found with a finger.

Silent Night

What should I wear today is not a question of faith. What should I wear today is the first thing you say upon rising, sad little loaf that you are. Some women pick at the skin on their lips, some women bite their nails or pull on their eyelashes like mulecarts trudging water to a refugee camp. I am talking around the fact that you aren't supposed to be here, in flesh or in my capacity to imagine my flesh as yours—touching me the way you would pull back the smallest bit of wick from a kerosene lantern. Make it fucking darker. Where is the mandarin robe flung across a chair-back & why can't my hands find it. Even under the full moon a body's outline is the amber gelatin a high school techie uses to clarify an actor's complexion on stage. Here, take this dim shell-light, Aphrodite with her perfect tousled look coming hither, grabbing her breast less for sexual effect than gravity. I swear I would run to you if not for these legs loping & coming back together as you might punch at the air in front of someones's face, then laugh generously. I swear I would run to you if you cried out from a dream & what you cried out was beauty, & the skeptical china hid again in cabinets, and the laundry folded its thin arms under its collars, & after touching me the world would end not with flood or fire or people throwing themselves out of buildings after breaking into Wal-Mart to steal electronic goods, no. The whole world & I might then sleep, sleep in heavenly peace.

Furniture Shopping

He said you don't have to go
to the grave to talk about
the grave.

The furniture in shambles.
The chair a stomach cramp.

What will you look like in fifty years
he mumbled, closer than me.

I don't care if the pencils are dull
I don't care if a partridge never gilds
the railing I don't care for all of the
crying babies I can't seemed like
the only reply.

It was new when we came by it.
Stained by which I mean several coats
laid down, warm and brown
laid down to him at once.

Tung oil. His mouth the burden
of several mouths debating.

What the hell am I doing.

He said a futon. He said minimalism.

Buffet armoire ottoman ten thousand
excited women at his feet. Later

Ataturk, loosed hair, educate me.
I will build the home I will die in
the home I will build.

Greenland

Dying is every yearbook signature squeaking: *see you at the beach!*, is a rubber Tomahawk with a feather the color of the air around a man your mother kisses, who is not your father at work in his office, picking up a paperweight, then putting that paperweight down solemnly. Dying is your boss chewing on a pen & counting with his fingers, then smiling with one side of his mouth, then counting with his fingers, & chewing on a pen. Dying is a woman so alone in a city that she does not think we see her adjusting her undergarments as she walks, head bent so that her hair falls across her face like the relief of driving snow just when you needed a reason to turn in for the night. Dying is a fold of children in 1928, whose Inuit mother with the help of her eldest daughter hangs them to end their misery of starvation. Dying is the eldest daughter, who then slips the noose around her own neck as you might put a motel key on a string to hang between your breasts in order to know where it is. Dying is how the ethnographer recorded the story, photographed it coolly—holding his own hand and turning on his heel from a crowd. Dying is the edge-curl of the photograph, which does not make the sound of those hardening bodies, broken teeth in a music box with a loose crank & a clown sadly peeling from the tin overlay. Dying is how we cannot stop looking at it.

Interrogation

Yes, if someone asked
and their eyes glinted flint
and their hands were a fire
at the edge of the Baltic
on a night when mothers
wolfed their children's rations
hurriedly under a spotlight
which was the only light
and then boarded a boxcar for Minsk—
If someone asked
right then, and if I were a reporter
and Spanish was my first language
and the question was translated to
me by a woman so beautiful
I pretended to be a man
swiping the dandruff from my suit
just to avoid the catechism of her eye
that would indicate every sin I did
and did not perform
though thought about nightly—
And if the question was worded
Did you really love him?
without a lilt at the end, rather
a dull thud like a flashlight
tossed into a river
in order to evade a bear
who was only interested in garbage,

I would have to say yes—
hands feeling around my clavicle
the way a woman with a pearl necklace
fondles that pearl necklace
except that I haven't got one,
and so lightly pinch at the skin
in a way that leaves a trail of red
inching toward my throat
which is slowly closing now
which is almost completely shut.

Application for Asylum

I am leaving this country, its name which eels me, sways me
       like my lover sways drunkard in the alley
I will leave the alley,   its festooned dumpsters,
       the girl body,
the hundreds of girls from small towns with their frosted lips
         & pity them.
Pity me, my fluoridated waters, my poison windowsills
           my gnashing children.
Pray you stay close to me in Wal-Mart,
         the biggest place I have been to date.
     To date you,
to clasp hands I abandon my right to wring hands,
       to lie down on the cold earth as though it were a belly
         against my cheek—
          the whip-kick inside the belly.

I am saying God, if you are anywhere, let you be an arctic night.
              I decamp the arctic night,
all nights I have loved the uncountable
      rivulets of your long robe.
         Undress me as I am fleeing the cloth.
File me so I might leave the nails and cut away my precious hair

Elegy for Guizhou

Three Gorges like 3 gorgeous.

The face a mother makes when imagining
her daughter's fist pushed
into anonymous slacks.

A man with no job to do
tying his shoelaces.

Sunrise over the wide Yangtze
away you rolling river.

There was nothing more we could do.

Away, bound away.

I don't want to be held
up by anything.

Stars as Comforting

Someone told you they heard
he went peacefully.

The stars' lassitude like a carpet
he trods on. Stars. Someone
doesn't say this.

Someone doesn't say:
impossible not to believe in light.
Unless you are blind.

He is not my brother he is
an asshole. I say and don't say
from time to time.

He is burnished. He is shooting.
He is shooting. Stars come
down. Pin me down. A million
silver thumb tacks.

I do say but I still love.
You say rub your eyes. Rub
the long night rub the silent
stars out of your eyes.

I thought I heard.

I prefer the stars honking,
like geese. Flapping. In the
confusion I will disappear,
you don't say. The sky above
will empty, empty of geese
you don't say.

How It Is I Am Married

Svalbard is my tiny gun. Night sets for approximately one month. We kiss all through the night; the sea laps like dogs who also kiss throughout the night. Svalbard remains to me a permanent pocket fixture. I touch its barrel, I cock it with one hand while my mouth laps like a woman with goiter laps salt from a smooth sea stone. Everything retracts, the cloudberries wither into malignant nodules, the snow is a low angry rime. We kiss permanently although it feels sudden, jet-streamed, and constantly I am reminded of my tiny gun that grows damp under the weight of my hand. We kiss under the damp weight of my hand. We kiss to keep our clothes on and do not tell anyone. We do not tell the bears, they have their own afflictions; I will lichen. Initially, our kiss will drive the bears away, it is so long and full of boots laced tightly. I am reminded to keep Svalbard tight against my thigh. Someday the bears are going to come for us. I will shoot my tiny gun into the night sky. Stars are nothing but fired bullets, I mean for them to take your breath away.

Leaving

I saw my dog with a limp bird
in her jaw and I knew the world
would end. Neither preceded the
dysfunction of this snow, darling.
When I lie down, I expect to be
covered up. The green ground.
Peter Freuchen ferried to me
is nodding and taking notes.
All the arctic explorers lacing up
their big dumb boots.
I mistook myself as someone
who could see the larger meaning
as the smallest vole occupies one-
third of my heart space.
The pattern of winter. The pattern
of frost on the pane. I remove
myself from beauty as the ethnographer's
sketch is crude and gloomy.
Feathers that are oily and full of mites
and snowing in, how you say, droves.
Is movement. Is rest.

Mother of Sadness

I had a little girl and I named
her Ada Blackjack.

I knew a tern and I killed
that tern not in a particularly
crude fashion, but not quickly,
either.

My legs are ruined and tethered
to a tree. There are tent
caterpillars everywhere.

They kicked me out of the tent.
The wind it is so fierce and
my little girl is in trouble.

Pinched a classmate.
Flung a rock at an eider duck.

All the folded notes of this world
one big love a sky doesn't
bother to contain. All my men
are fools.

O, my blood is black
the night. The middle of
the day. A bird could

land on my voice's wire line:

Give me a whistle.

Economics Theory

You look up at the procession of clouds and say, my heart is break-ing. A child who slips a satchel onto a stick and sets off with a single can of beans is breaking. The radio is broken. The crackle it emits shakes the eaves where a pigeon roosts trying to mend its wing. The red paint on the schoolhouse is peeling. The lunchlady inside wipes the sweat from her brow with rags torn from an old towel. She rips a head of lettuce into a plastic bowl like she is gesturing to you to come see what she has in her van, which turns out to be nothing, really, except for a man in the backseat smiling with half of his face. He may or may not break you as it would break you to lose your favorite tree in the yard, or it may improve the view, which in turn increases the value of your prop-erty. Whatever is demanded you must supply, it is economics—in some cases you will go broke either way if you are not careful to price some people out. Have a good cry for the poor; their bitten nails and hoarse voices will not be tendered. Remind them to keep their mouths shut. Stenosis is dealt with in one of two ways: the heart valve is replaced with a mechanical valve, or cut, short-ened, separated, made stronger. In both cases the heart must not beat. A woman in the hospital waiting room is reading an article on celebrity break-ups while she waits for news from the doctor. Who is going to be OK. Who is going to turn out just fine.

Afterhours

It is late and the waitress is shining cutlery, folding cloth squares into neat little tents a boy who is small for his age might imagine sleeping under. Each table a fabled island. Fertile the way boys cry in swaths bundled from a scythe; a narrow plot, cleared. You approach the restaurant as you assume your mother must approach your laundry when you have not lived with your mother for many years. Load after load, a small feast of you. You break camp, lay the napkin flat like a palm against your crotch. Your meal, unremarkable, California Cuisine with Italian accents. Sicily is an island where noodles are thrown against the escarpment like what-I-could-do-to-you letters. Where are heart and soul hanging out, someone singing sweetly, someone picturing you in your undecorated room eating from a bag. Men cry in leftovers, cry in Hep B abandoned on a fork. All the scraping and scraping into trash bins. The waitress just misses pretty, but is fastidious and keeps her eyes low. Will there be anything else? Her sidework is every way we organize sadness, drawers of it we ask others to pay for. The desserts offered are too beautiful. No, nothing else

thank-you.

About the Author

Paige Ackerson Kiely currently resides in Lincoln, Vermont where she works as a clerk and tends her family.

Ahsahta Press

SAWTOOTH POETRY PRIZE SERIES

2002: Aaron McCollough, *Welkin* (Brenda Hillman, judge)

2003: Graham Foust, *Leave the Room to Itself* (Joe Wenderoth, judge)

2004: Noah Eli Gordon, *The Area of Sound Called the Subtone* (Claudia Rankine, judge)

2005: Karla Kelsey, *Knowledge, Forms, The Aviary* (Carolyn Forché, judge)

2006: Paige Ackerson-Kiely, *In No One's Land* (D. A. Powell, judge)

2007: Rusty Morrison, *the true keeps calm biding its story* (Peter Gizzi, judge)

2008: Barbara Maloutas, *the whole Marie* (C. D. Wright, judge)

NEW SERIES

1. Lance Phillips, *Corpus Socius*
2. Heather Sellers, *Drinking Girls and Their Dresses*
3. Lisa Fishman, *Dear, Read*
4. Peggy Hamilton, *Forbidden City*
5. Dan Beachy-Quick, *Spell*
6. Liz Waldner, *Saving the Appearances*
7. Charles O. Hartman, *Island*
8. Lance Phillips, *Cur aliquid vidi*
9. Sandra Miller, *oriflamme.*
10. Brigitte Byrd, *Fence Above the Sea*
11. Ethan Paquin, *The Violence*
12. Ed Allen, *67 Mixed Messages*
13. Brian Henry, *Quarantine*
14. Kate Greenstreet, *case sensitive*
15. Aaron McCollough, *Little Ease*
16. Susan Tichy, *Bone Pagoda*
17. Susan Briante, *Pioneers in the Study of Motion*
18. Lisa Fishman, *The Happiness Experiment*
19. Heidi Lynn Staples, *Dog Girl*
20. David Mutschlecner, *Sign*
21. Kristi Maxwell, *Realm Sixty-four*
22. G. E. Patterson, *To and From*
23. Chris Vitiello, *Irresponsibility*
24. Stephanie Strickland, *Zone : Zero*
25. Charles O. Hartman, *New and Selected Poems*
26. Kath Jesme, *The Plum-Stone Game*
27. Ben Doller, *FAQ:*
28. Carrie Olivia Adams, *Intervening Absence*
29. Rachel Loden, *Dick of the Dead*

Ahsahta Press

MODERN AND CONTEMPORARY
POETRY OF THE AMERICAN WEST

This book is set in Apollo MT type with Bauer Bodoni titles
by Ahsahta Press at Boise State University.
Cover design by Quemadura.
Book design by Janet Holmes.

AHSAHTA PRESS
2007

JANET HOLMES, DIRECTOR
CHRISTOPHER KLINGBEIL
ERIK LEAVITT
JANNA VEGA
ALLISON VON MAUR
ABIGAIL L. WOLFORD